The Hodder Wayland Boo

Common British Mammals

A Photographic Guide

Shirley Thompson

HODDER
Wayland

an imprint of Hodder Children's Books

The Wayland Book of
Common British Mammals
A Photographic Guide

Front cover picture: A fox picks up a scent trail.

Title page picture: A stoat climbs down a tree with ease.

Contents page pictures (from top): Wood mouse; noctule bat; roe deer; domestic cat

Designer: Victoria Webb

Produced for Wayland Publishers Ltd by
Roger Coote Publishing
Gissing's Farm, Fressingfield
Suffolk IP21 5SH, England

Printed in Hong Kong by Wing King Tong Co Ltd

First published in Great Britain in 1998
by Wayland Publishers Ltd

This paperback edition published in 2000 by Hodder Wayland,
an imprint of Hodder Children s Books

Reprinted in 2002.

© Hodder Wayland 1998

British Library Cataloguing in Publication Data
Thompson, Shirley
The Wayland Book of Common British Mammals:
A Photographic Guide
1. Mammals – Great Britain – Juvenile literature 2. Mammals –
Great Britain – Pictorial works – Juvenile literature
I. Title II. Common British mammals.
599'.0941

ISBN 0 7502 2829 6

**All Wayland books encourage children to read
and help them improve their literacy.**

✓ The contents page, page numbers, headings and index help locate specific pieces of information.

✓ The glossary reinforces alphabetic knowledge and extends vocabulary.

✓ The further information section suggests other books dealing with the same subject.

Picture acknowledgements
Bruce Coleman Collection *front cover* (Hans Reinhard), 9 bottom (Jane Burton), 12 (Jens Rydell), 19 bottom (Jane Burton), 27 (Hans Reinhard), 28 bottom (Hans Reinhard); Frank Lane Picture Agency 1 (R Tidman), 19 top (R Wilmshurst), 23 bottom (R P Lawrence), 28 top (R Tidman), 29 (D A Robinson), 41 top (Michael Callan), 45 (Foto Natura); Papilio Photographic 4 top (Neil Miller), 5 (Robert Pickett), 6 (Jamie Harron), 7 (William Dunn), 8 (Steve Austin), 10 left (Steve Austin), 10 top (Alastair Shay), 11 (Alastair Shay), 13 (Alastair Shay), 14 (William Middleton), 15 (Michael Maconachie), 16 (Robert Pickett), 17 (Laura Sivell), 18 (Steve Austin), 20 (Mike Buxton), 21 (Chris Beddall), 22 (Ken Wilson), 23 top (Chris Beddall), 26 (Clive Druett), 30 (Robert Pickett), 31 (David Smith), 32 (Dr Philip Marazzi), 33 (Alastair Shay), 34 (Brian Knox), 35 left (Annie Poole), 35 right (David Smith), 36 (Clive Druett), 37 top (Jane Sweeney), 38 top (Ken Wilson), 38 bottom (Michael Maconachie), 39 top (Clive Druett), 39 bottom (Robert Gill), 40 right (Clive Druett), 41 bottom (Robert Pickett), 46 (Clive Druett); Touchstone Images 4 bottom, 40 left; University of Aberdeen 24 (Ben Wilson); Wayland Picture Library 37 bottom; Zefa 9 top, 25. All maps and artwork on page 42 by Victoria Webb. Artwork on pages 43, 44 and 45 by Peter Bull.

Contents

Introduction

Mammals are very special animals. They are a varied group that includes creatures as different as elephants and squirrels, as well as cats, dogs and humans. Although they are so different from one another, mammals all share some characteristics. For example, all mammals have some hair or fur on their bodies and they are all warm-blooded. The main feature that sets them apart from other types of animals is that, instead of laying eggs, they give birth to young which the mother feeds on milk from her mammary glands.

There are about 4,500 different species of mammal in the world. They live in just about every habitat you can think of – from gerbils in the hot desert to polar bears in the arctic. Sixty-four species of land mammal live in Britain and over 20 marine mammals visit the seas around our coasts.

Below: This Jersey cow provides exactly the right milk for her calf to grow well.

This book will introduce you to some of our most common wild mammals. However, the word 'common' can mean different things. For example, some mammals are widespread, living in almost every part of Britain. Some live only in particular habitats, whilst others may be seen in very large numbers in only one or two parts of the country.

We rarely see wild mammals, as most are shy and many are nocturnal, which means they are only active at night. Sadly, the only time most people see a fox or a badger is when it has been hit by a car on the road. Other smaller mammals, such as wood mice or bats, may be brought into the house by cats. But by learning to recognize mammals' tracks and trails, you are more likely to find these animals in the wild. At the end of this book are hints for spotting the signs that tell you which animal has passed by. If you are lucky enough to spot wild mammals, the pictures and the sizes given in this book should help you to identify them. But remember that the sizes given for the animals are only a rough guide, as they can vary a good deal.

Above: The common seal is the most widespread of all seals.

Common seals

Maps
For each of the wild mammals in this book there is a map to show where it lives. For example, the map on the right illustrates where common seals are found. The coloured shading shows the animal's main range – where it usually lives and breeds. It may also live outside that area, but that would be rare.

Hedgehog

The hedgehog is the only prickly mammal in Britain. Some of the hairs on its back are sharp spines, which are creamy brown with dark tips. Underneath it has soft fur that hides quite long legs. When it is alarmed, a hedgehog will curl up into a ball, and raise up its spines to protect itself.

Hedgehogs live where there is grassland near woods or hedges, and they often visit people's gardens. They can travel up to 3 km a night looking for food – mainly caterpillars, earthworms and slugs.

In June, the female gives birth to between three and five babies in a nest of leaves and grass. She may have a second litter later in the year. Hedgehogs hibernate from October to April. They make winter nests in piles of dry leaves or straw, or even in garden compost heaps. People can help hedgehogs by not clearing away all the leaves that fall in their gardens in autumn. It is also a good idea to check any bonfire before lighting it, in case there is a hibernating hedgehog underneath.

Hedgehogs

Top: Hedgehogs are most often seen at dawn or at dusk.

Mole

Moles have short, velvety fur, tiny eyes the size of pinheads, and a long, sensitive nose. They live almost anywhere the soil is deep enough for them to dig tunnels with their spade-like front feet. When moles dig, they push the loosened soil up a shaft to the surface, forming piles of earth called molehills. It is easy to see these in fields and gardens.

A mole patrols its tunnel regularly to see what has fallen in, looking especially for earthworms – its favourite foods – and insects. Its fur brushes in any direction, so the mole can run backwards through its tunnel. When moving backwards, it holds its short, whiskered tail upright and uses it to feel its way along.

During April or May, female moles have three or four babies in a nest of dry leaves and grass. When the young are weaned and leave the nest, they must travel on the surface to find a new home. This is a very dangerous time for them, as they risk being caught and eaten by predators such as tawny owls and stoats.

■ **Moles**

Below: Moles spend most of their time underground. This one has just pushed its way to the surface.

Common Shrew

Head and body 75 mm long,
tail 35 mm long

The common shrew is one of three main species of shrew in Britain. All three have a pointed snout, small eyes, rounded ears and long whiskers. Shrews have short legs and short fur.

The common shrew has a dark brown back, a pale belly, and mid-brown sides, or flanks. It lives among thick grass, bushes and hedgerows. It cannot see very well, but its senses of smell, touch and hearing are good. It pushes its long snout into the soil or fallen leaves, searching for beetles, spiders and other invertebrates.

Common shrews are very aggressive creatures, and they live alone except when bringing up young. Their nests are made of dried grass and leaves, and are made underground or under logs.

■ **Common shrews**

Females have two litters each year. When they are born, the babies are completely blind and have no fur.

Below: In summer you may hear a common shrew twittering as it searches for food.

Shrews use up energy so quickly that they have to feed day and night, resting only briefly from time to time.

Pygmy Shrew

Head and body 50 mm long, tail 40 mm long

The pygmy shrew is smaller than the common shrew, but has a longer, thicker tail. It is a medium brown colour, with a dirty white belly. Pygmy shrews live wherever there is plenty of ground cover to hide them from predators such as owls, foxes and domestic cats. They make runways through moss and grass, darting very fast over the ground. Dead common and pygmy shrews are sometimes found on paths, killed by a predator but left uneaten because they taste very unpleasant.

Unlike common shrews, pygmy shrews do not dig for food and they eat smaller prey, especially woodlice.

Above: Although they are found over a larger area than common shrews, there are fewer pygmy shrews in Britain than common shrews.

■ **Pygmy shrews**

Water Shrew

Head and body 85 mm long, tail 65 mm long

It is easy to tell the water shrew from other shrews, as it is larger, has a black back and is silvery grey underneath.

Water shrews swim and dive well, and they usually live on the banks of clean, fast-flowing rivers and streams. They hunt both on land and underwater, sometimes catching prey larger than themselves. In the water they catch invertebrates, especially freshwater shrimps, and small fish. On land they eat mainly beetles, spiders and earthworms.

Water shrews live in burrows which they dig in the banks of streams. The entrance to the burrow is normally above the water level. One or two litters of about six young are raised each year in a nest of moss, grass and small stones inside the burrow.

■ **Water shrews**

Left: The water shrew uses all four legs to 'doggy-paddle' under the water.

Pipistrelle Bat

Head and body 40 mm long,
wing span 220 mm long

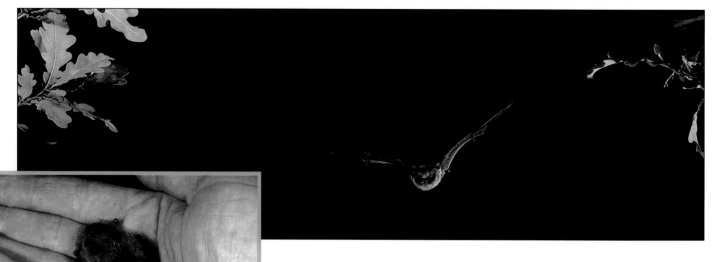

The pipistrelle is the smallest of the 16 species of bat that breed in Britain. There are actually two species of common pipistrelle, but it is very difficult to tell them apart.

Pipistrelles share many of the characteristics of the other British bat species. For example, although they occasionally fly during the day, you are most likely to see them at dusk. They are all insect-eaters, and they hunt their prey using a sonar system called echolocation. Bats send out a series of high-pitched squeaks and clicks. When these sounds strike an insect they bounce back. The bat can then find its prey.

In order to survive, bats need lots of food. They also need a variety of places in which to live, as they choose different roosting places during the year. Their natural homes are trees and caves, but many bats have also learned to live in buildings, under bridges and in other places that have been built by people.

In spring, pregnant female bats gather in a warm place to give birth to their young. Each female usually has only one baby in a year. The babies cannot fly for at least three weeks. The group stays together until autumn when the young are able to catch their own food. Then they move away and separate. In winter, bats hibernate in a cool, safe place.

Pipistrelles twist and turn as they fly in woodland glades, over water and around street lights. Being so small, they need to eat tiny insects like midges, and may catch as many as 3,000 in a night.

**Above: A pipistrelle bat in flight.
Inset: An adult pipistrelle, with its wings folded, is so small that it would fit into a matchbox.**

■ Pipistrelle bats

Like us, bats have two legs and two arms. But the bones of their fingers are very long and they act as a frame for the wing membrane. Bats are the only mammals that can fly — and they do so with their hands!

Brown Long-eared Bat

Head and body 45 mm long, wing span 250 mm long

These bats have fluffy fur, and huge ears, which they fold away when they are resting. They usually live near areas of woodland, where they flit through the branches of the trees and snatch insects from the leaves.

Long-eared bats come out after dark. They keep close to trees as they fly, which means that they are very difficult to spot. If you are lucky, you may to see one hovering near night-scented flowers such as honeysuckle, waiting to pounce on moths that are feeding there.

There are 16 species of bat that live in Britain; some of them are very rare. They are: the greater horseshoe, lesser horseshoe, whiskered, Brandt's, Natterer's, Bechstein's, Daubenton's, serotine, noctule, Leisler's, two species of common pipistrelle, Nathusius's pipistrelle, barbastelle, brown long-eared and grey long-eared bat.

Brown long-eared bats

Below: See how large this long-eared bat's ears are, compared to the size of its head.

Daubenton's Bat

Head and body 50 mm long, wing span 250 mm

Daubenton's bats usually feed over water. They fly close to the surface, looking like little hovercraft. Unlike pipistrelles, they fly very directly instead of flitting here and there. They circle again and again where insects gather, catching them with their large feet or scooping them up with their tail membrane.

There is a good chance of seeing Daubenton's bats over lakes, rivers and canals shortly after sunset.

■ **Daubenton's bats**

Left: A Daubenton's bat leaves an old mine, where it has been hibernating.

Today there are fewer bats than there were in the past. Birds of prey catch some, and cats often kill or injure bats. But people are the real problem. We have damaged or destroyed many of the places where bats used to feed or roost. The pesticides we use have killed the insects that bats feed on, as well as many of the bats themselves.

Noctule Bat

Head and body 75 mm long, wing span 375 mm

Noctules are among Britain's largest bats. They are often called tree bats, because they roost in holes in large trees. Their sleek fur and long, narrow wings make them very streamlined and capable of flying fast.

Noctules come out early in the evening while it is still light. They may travel several kilometres to their feeding ground, flying high in a straight line and then swooping down on their insect prey.

 **Noctule bats**

Above: Large old trees, including dead ones, are very important as roosting sites for noctule bats.

13

Rabbit

Head and body 440 mm long, ear length 70 mm

The rabbit is familiar to everyone, with its soft, greyish-brown fur and long, black whiskers. Rabbits constantly listen and watch for danger with their long ears and large eyes. When alarmed they thump the ground with their hind feet to warn others of danger, especially predators such as foxes, stoats and domestic cats.

Rabbits were first brought to Britain about 900 years ago by the Normans, who kept them for meat and fur. Although they were kept in enclosed warrens, many rabbits escaped and lived in the wild.

You may see rabbits feeding anywhere there is short grass with hiding places such as hedges nearby. They eat grasses, young leaves and shoots, leaving the grass short as if cut by a lawnmower. Many rabbits live in colonies in a system of burrows called a warren, which has several entrances.

The female rabbit, or doe, makes a nest of grass and moss. She lines the nest with fur plucked from her belly. A doe may have several litters in a year – giving birth to as many as 20 young altogether. She visits her young once each evening to suckle them, blocking the burrow entrance with soil and plants while she is away. By the time they are four months old the young rabbits are themselves able to breed.

Rabbits

Top: This rabbit has found some juicy plums to eat.

Brown Hare

Head and body 540 mm long, ear length 100 mm

The brown hare is larger than the rabbit. It is brownish in colour and has long legs and long, black-tipped ears. It does not live underground, so if you see one it will gallop away rather than dashing into a burrow. Hares can run very fast.

Hares are normally nocturnal, but it is quite common to see them in the morning and evening during summer. The brown hare is most common in areas of farmland, especially where cereal crops such as wheat are grown. They feed on these crops, particularly when the plants are young. However, they prefer to eat wild grasses and herbs if they can.

Hares breed almost all year round – occasionally even in winter. Males sometimes compete with each other for a particular female, chasing and biting until one gives up. They are also seen 'boxing' one another, although this usually happens between a male and a female who does not want to mate. A female may have about three litters of young in a year. Each litter has from one to four babies, which are called leverets.

Bottom: In recent years, brown hares have become quite rare in much of Britain.

Brown hares

15

Grey Squirrel

Grey squirrels

In summer grey squirrels build nests, or dreys, which consist of shallow platforms of twigs among the branches of trees. Each year they raise one or two litters of three or four young. They do not hibernate in winter. Instead they store food, and build a large winter nest close to the trunk of a tree, which several animals will share. Grey squirrels have few predators, but many are killed on the roads.

Below: Grey Squirrels spend a lot of time on the ground. They can often be seen out in the open, searching for food.

In summer the grey squirrel has yellowish-brown fur that moults to silvery grey in autumn. Its bushy tail is grey. It has strong feet and sharp claws that help it to climb trees and walls.

Grey squirrels are common in woodlands, and they also live in parks, gardens and even towns where there are trees and hedges. They are easy to watch and may take food from a bird table or even from your hand. They eat nuts and seeds, as well as fungi, shoots and tree bark.

Although the grey squirrel is one of the most familiar wild mammals in Britain, it is not a native. It was first brought here from Canada and the USA just over 100 years ago, and released in many places in England and Wales, and later in Scotland. Grey squirrels are now a serious pest in some places as they damage growing trees.

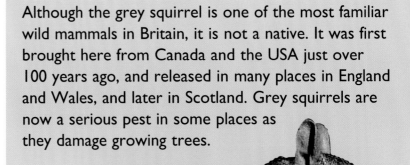

Red Squirrel

Red squirrels

This is our only native squirrel. It was once common over most of England and Wales. Now it is found in only a few places, mainly near large areas of coniferous forest. It spends most of its time in trees. The red squirrel is slightly smaller than the grey squirrel, with bright chestnut-coloured fur in the summer, ear tufts and a bushy tail.

The red squirrel eats nuts, acorns, berries and the cones of conifers. During late summer and autumn, red squirrels store food in holes just under the surface of the soil. These stores are dug up and eaten during the winter. In areas where food is scarce, red squirrels are not able to compete with their grey cousins.

Red squirrels spend much of their time on their own, but they do sometimes share nests, especially in winter and spring. Their nests, or dreys, are spherical and about 30 cm across. They are made of twigs lined with moss, leaves and bark. Dreys are built close to the trunks of trees, at least 6 m above the ground.

The breeding season can last from December through to the following September. A female has one or two litters in a year, each with between one and six young. When they are born, red squirrels are blind, deaf and have no fur. By the time they are about 7 weeks old, they start leaving their nest and eating solid food.

Above: Red squirrels leap from tree to tree and rarely come down to the ground.

Bank Vole

At first sight, voles are similar to mice. But, unlike mice they are chubby, with round faces, blunt noses and small eyes and ears. Voles have a long, shaggy coat, short legs and a short tail.

The bank vole has chestnut fur on its back, with silvery grey underneath. Its tail is half the length of its head and body. Bank voles live in woods where there are plenty of shrubs or plants under the trees, or near bramble thickets. Where there is cover they use runways above ground, and are active both day and night. Their favourite foods are fleshy fruits and seeds, but they will also eat leaves, fungi and invertebrates such as worms. In late autumn bank voles store food, and during winter they will eat dead leaves.

In summer the bank vole builds a breeding nest of leaves, moss and feathers, either below ground or above in the tree trunks. If there is plenty of food, voles may raise several litters, but many will die in bad weather. Many more become food for tawny owls, weasels, foxes and other predators.

Bank voles

Top: This bank vole has found a tasty hazelnut to eat.

There are three species of vole in Britain – the bank vole, the field vole and the water vole.

Field Vole

Head and body 110 mm long, tail 40 mm long

Sometimes called the short-tailed vole, the field vole is very similar to the bank vole, except that it has greyish-brown fur. Its tail is a third the length of its head and body.

The field vole is thought to be our commonest mammal, and there are an estimated 75 million of them in Britain. It makes runways through the long, rough grass where it prefers to live, and builds its nest in a clump of grass or under a log. Grass is the field vole's main food: it enjoys the juicy lower part of the stems, but will also eat roots and leaves. This vole is usually nocturnal in summer, but is most active at dawn and dusk. The females give birth to several litters of young through the summer.

The field vole is hunted by many predators including barn owls, kestrels and stoats.

■ **Field voles**

Left: Field voles can live in narrow strips of grassland next to roads.

Water Vole

Head and body 200 mm long, tail 120 mm long

The water vole is the largest British vole. It has dark brown or black fur and is about the same size as a rat. However, the water vole has a rounder body, a chubbier face and a shorter tail than the rat.

Water voles rarely venture far from water. They prefer clean, slow-moving water with lots of plants on the banks. They live in burrows, sometimes with entrances below the waterline, and make nests of shredded grass and reeds. Water voles can be seen during the day feeding on waterside plants, sitting on their hind feet and holding a stalk in their front paws. There is a distinct 'plop' when one dives into the water. As it swims you can see its nose above the water, and a V-shaped wake behind it.

Above: Water voles are often mistakenly called water rats. The character Ratty in Kenneth Graham's *The Wind in the Willows* is actually a water vole.

■ **Water voles**

Common Rat

Head and body 250 mm long,
tail 220 mm long

The common or brown rat has shaggy fur, which is grey-brown on its back and pale grey on its belly. It has a more pointed muzzle than the water vole, with bigger eyes and ears and a long, scaly tail.

Common rats usually live near buildings – especially on farms, in refuse dumps or in warehouses. They often dig burrows beside ditches, leaving heaps of earth nearby. Unlike water voles, rats can live in polluted water, even in sewers, and they slip into the water without making any sound.

Rats will eat many things, from cereals, bones and root crops to earthworms.

Common rats

In towns, rats live in large colonies that are made up of many small groups, or 'clans'. As they become more crowded, each clan's territory becomes smaller and smaller. The most powerful, high-ranking males, choose the best territories, nearest their source of food.

Rats live in colonies, in long burrow systems with many exits, and usually make their nests below ground. They breed throughout the year, raising litters of seven or eight young.

The common rat is a serious pest, as it destroys stored food, and carries diseases that infect people and other animals. Cats and foxes may hunt young rats, but adults are usually too fierce for most predators to catch.

Below: Common rats first arrived in Britain less than 250 years ago. Since then, they have spread wherever food is easy to find.

Wood Mouse

The wood mouse is also known as the long-tailed field mouse. It has a sandy-brown back and a pale grey or white belly. It lives in fields and gardens as well as in woods, and may come into buildings where it is often mistaken for a house mouse. Seeds are its main food, but it eats many other things, such as buds and worms.

Wood mice live in a group in a burrow system. Their nests of leaves and moss are usually below ground, often under roots of trees or shrubs.

■ **Wood mice**

Above: A wood mouse eating catkins.

House Mouse

Western house mice

Eastern house mice

Scientists have discovered recently that there are actually two different species of house mouse in Europe. The eastern house mouse is very slightly larger than the western house mouse and has a shorter tail.

House mice are dull grey-brown on their back and sides and paler below. Compared with wood mice, they have a thicker, more scaly tail, smaller eyes and ears, and shorter hind feet.

They are common near buildings – especially where food is stored – and will eat almost anything. They are particularly fond of cereal grains. They often make their nests under floors or behind skirting boards. A female can raise up to 50 young in a year.

House mice are serious pests. They spoil stored grain and other food. Rats, cats, owls and small meat-eating mammals all prey on wood mice and house mice.

Above: This western house mouse has chewed its way through a skirting board.

Harvest Mouse

Head and body 65 mm long, tail 65 mm long

The harvest mouse is the smallest of the mice that live in Britain. It has a russet-orange back and a white belly, and its ears are smaller than those of other species of mice. The harvest mouse usually lives in tall plants such as long grass and reeds, and grasps the stalks with its long tail as it climbs. Its diet includes seeds, insects and fungi.

Although they are mainly nocturnal in winter, harvest mice are active in daylight during summer. However, they are extremely shy and are hardly ever seen by people.

■ **Harvest mice**

Left: This harvest mouse has found a meal of seeds.

Dormouse

Head and body 80 mm long, tail 65 mm long

The dormouse is the only mouse-sized mammal that has a long furry tail. Adults are bright golden-brown. They live in deciduous woodland where there is plenty of undergrowth, and they spend most of the summer in trees. Their diet changes through the year, from flowers in spring to fruit and berries in autumn.

In summer dormice make woven nests in bushes or trees, but they hibernate in winter nests under leaves at ground level. The common dormouse is much less common than it used to be.

■ **Dormice**

Far left: Dormice may spend up to nine months of the year in hibernation.

Harbour Porpoise

Harbour porpoises and bottlenose dolphins belong to a group of mammals called cetaceans. They have a thick layer of blubber below the skin that keeps them warm. They hold their breath to dive, coming to the surface to breathe through a blowhole, an opening at the top of their head.

The harbour porpoise is the smallest British cetacean. It has a chunky shape, with no forehead or 'beak' on its small head. It rarely leaps out of the water, but the triangular dorsal fin in the middle of its back can be seen just above the surface. Harbour porpoises look dark grey but they have paler patches on their flanks and a white belly. Porpoises eat fish, including herring, mackerel and whiting, as well as squid and cuttlefish.

Harbour porpoises are not easy to spot as they show very little of their body above the water. They are usually seen alone or in small groups of up to 10. They are most often seen near the coast, within about 10 km of land. They breathe frequently, coming to the surface with a slow, rolling movement. Sometimes you might hear them blow to get rid of the stale air in their lungs. When they do this they make a sound rather like a sneeze.

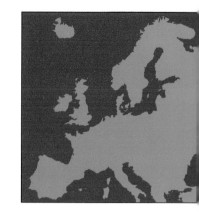

Harbour porpoises

Below: A harbour porpoise is rescued after it became stranded in shallow water.

Bottlenose Dolphin

The bottlenose dolphin has a torpedo-shaped body with a short 'beak' on its head. Its back is brown or dark grey, with lighter grey flanks and a white belly. The young, called calves, are paler than the adults. The flippers of the bottlenose dolphin are dark and fairly long, and its dorsal fin is sickle-shaped and more slender than that of the porpoise.

These dolphins often leap out of water. Sometimes they are seen 'bow-riding' – surfing along on the pressure wave that travels through the water in front of a moving boat.

They eat a variety of fish including salmon and cod, as well as squid and cuttlefish. They usually feed alone or in small groups, sometimes herding fish together to make them easier to catch. The best chance of sighting bottlenose dolphins is from July to September, swimming alone or in groups of up to 50, but you may see them at any time of the year.

Bottlenose dolphins

Above: A bottlenose dolphin leaps clear of the water. Female bottlenose dolphins may live to 50 years of age.

Fox

Most people would immediately recognize a fox if they saw one for the first time, with its orange-red fur, bushy tail or 'brush' and black socks. But, foxes are smaller than most people imagine – not much bigger than a domestic cat.

Foxes live almost anywhere there is cover and plenty of food. They are not fussy feeders, and will take whatever they can. In summer they catch rabbits, mice and voles, pigeons, earthworms and lots of beetles. In autumn they will eat fallen apples and blackberries. They also scavenge, especially in winter, taking food and other leftovers from dustbins. When it is hunting, a fox walks along slowly, then pounces on its prey and snaps at it with its long jaws.

Foxes are mainly nocturnal, and often show up in the car headlights at night. They may rest by day on a low roof or under a garden shed.

Above: A fox on the prowl. Foxes are successful because they will eat almost anything.

Many foxes live in towns and cities. They often visit gardens where they search for scraps.

However, it is not unusual to see them moving about in the day.

Foxes are sociable animals, and family groups share a territory. The dog (male) and vixen (female) mate for life, breeding only once a year. The vixen digs an earth where her litter of four or five cubs is born in March. At first they are blind and deaf, and the vixen stays with them for two or three weeks. During this time the dog fox brings her food. After a few weeks the young cubs make their first trip outside. Other females who have not had young may help look after them. The family hunts and plays together until the autumn, when some of the young move away to find new territory of their own.

■ **Foxes**

Below: Foxes mark the boundaries of their territory with scent so that other foxes can recognize it.

Stoat

The stoat has a long, slender body and short legs. It has very long whiskers, a black, dog-like muzzle and short, rounded ears. Its fur is a ginger-brown colour above and creamy below, with a black tip to its tail. In the north, the stoat's fur turns white in winter, except for the tip of its tail.

Stoats live anywhere there is cover and food. This may be farmland, woodland, marsh or mountain. They may make their dens in rock crevices or in empty rabbit burrows. As a stoat moves along swiftly, it bounds and gallops, arching its back, following hedges and stone walls to avoid open spaces. It climbs well and can run along branches and head-first down tree trunks.

The stoat is a fierce predator. It searches for voles, mice and other small mammals using its keen hearing and sight. When it spots potential prey, the stoat chases quickly after it, following its scent. It kills with a swift bite at the back of the neck. If food is short stoats will eat earthworms and fruit.

Left: A stoat creeps towards a nest, in search of a meal.

Stoats

Below: A stoat in its white winter coat is called an ermine.

Weasel

From a distance a weasel looks very like a stoat, with ginger-brown fur on its back. However, the weasel is smaller, its belly is white and it has a shorter tail than the stoat with no black tip. In the countryside, you might occasionally see a stoat or a weasel streaking across the road, its legs moving so fast that they look blurred.

The weasel's habitat is very wide, but it is less common on higher mountains and open woodland than the stoat, and is not found in Ireland. It hunts in a similar way to the stoat, but it also searches the runways of mice and voles. It can live for months in a mouse-infested stack of straw bales, eating its way through the other residents. The weasel has a good sense of hearing, sight and smell. It climbs and swims well and sometimes raids bird nest boxes. Weasels make a nest of leaves in a hole or crevice.

Weasels

Top: When marking their territory, weasels and stoats produce a very strong scent.

29

Mink

Head and body 375 mm long, tail 170 mm long

The mink is a medium-sized mammal, smaller than the average cat, with a pointed face, chocolate-brown fur and a slightly bushy tail.

Mink are regularly seen during the day, most often by rivers and streams with bankside cover, lakes with reed beds, or on undisturbed rocky coasts. A mink may use several dens, often beside waterside trees, or in rabbit burrows, usually within 10 m of the water's edge. Mink bound along, and climb and swim well. They use all four limbs when they are swimming underwater, but only the front limbs when they are paddling along at the surface.

Mink hunt on the ground, down burrows and even up trees, and they catch a wide range of prey. Rabbits are their main food. They catch ducks and moorhens on rivers and lakes, and gulls on the coast. They also catch slow-moving fish such as eels and crayfish.

The mink that live in Britain are actually called American mink. They were first brought here in 1929 and bred for their fur. All the wild mink in Britain are descended from animals that escaped or were released from fur farms.

 Mink

Top: Mink are very curious animals. They seem not to be afraid of people.

Otter

The otter is larger than the largest domestic cat. It has a flattened head, small eyes and ears, and a broad muzzle. The otter's fur is lighter than that of a mink, and its tail is longer and very thick at the base. When it swims, only its head shows above water, making a large, V-shaped wake.

Otters always live by water – lakes, marshes, rivers or coasts. They are nocturnal except on the coast, and are a very rare sight. Their resting places, called holts, are beneath piles of sticks or under tree roots. When they swim on the surface of the water they kick with all four feet, but underwater they use their whole body. Otters eat mostly fish, chasing them fast underwater. They also catch crayfish, frogs and occasionally even rabbits.

Otter numbers began to fall from 1957 onwards, and many people blamed this on the increasing use of pesticides to kill insects on farm crops. The pesticides found their way into rivers and streams, and poisoned the fish and the otters themselves. Now more effort is made to prevent these chemicals polluting rivers, and the otter's habitat is protected. As a result, otters are returning to our rivers.

Otters

Below: Otters are not often seen because they are very shy and avoid people.

Badger

Everyone knows the badger, with its striped head and grizzled grey body. But, few people have ever seen a badger in the wild, as they are nocturnal and very shy. Badgers live in hedgerows, open fields and even under buildings, but they are most at home in woodland. They need well-drained soil that is easy to dig in, and a good supply of food nearby.

A badger's sense of smell is hundreds of times better than ours. As they feed, badgers probe the ground with their strong, flexible snout. They will eat all sorts of food, from insects to fruit and young rabbits to hedgehogs, but earthworms are their favourites.

Badgers have no natural predators, but many are killed crossing roads. They still follow their old paths that were made long before the roads were built.

Badgers live in large groups, usually one or two families together. Their home is a network of tunnels and chambers called a sett, with up to 10 entrances. Badgers line the chambers with grass and leaves and clean them out often, shuffling out of the tunnel backwards pulling the bedding along with their front paws. Badgers groom very thoroughly, using their claws and teeth to groom each other as well as themselves.

On the surface, pathways between entrances and feeding places are well-worn by generations of badgers. When feeding and foraging, they walk slowly, though when alarmed, they run fast and can also swim and climb. To help them recognize places and other members of their group, badgers mark their territory and each other with scent from a special gland.

Above: Although they live in groups, badgers usually feed alone. They smack their lips noisily as they eat.

 Badgers

One or two young, called cubs, are born in February. They have pink skin, greyish-silver fur and their eye stripe is already showing. The cubs stay below ground for eight weeks. From April they come out each evening, and enjoy playing, chasing and jumping on each other. Badgers don't hibernate in the winter. However, they will stay underground for a long time in cold weather, living off fat that they have stored in their bodies.

Below: Badgers mark each other with their scent. All the badgers in a group can then recognize each other by smell.

Common Seal

Two species of seal – the common or harbour seal and the grey or Atlantic seal – are seen regularly around British coasts, and they are not easy to tell apart. They can be seen most clearly when they have hauled themselves out of the water, on rocks, or at low tide on sand banks. Sometimes they will 'bottle' in the water, holding their body upright with their face just showing above the surface. They can dive to a great depth and stay underwater for a long time.

The hair of common seals can vary in colour from black to grey or sandy brown, generally speckled with small, dark spots. This seal has a small head, which is rounded at the top.

Common seals eat many different species of fish, catching

Below: A common seal rests on some rocks.

whatever is plentiful at the time. Their whiskers are very sensitive and can detect vibrations in the water caused by fish swimming. The seals can also see and hear well underwater. When they catch their prey, they swallow it whole.

The female has one baby, or pup, each year, in June or early July. She gives birth on rocks or sand banks. The pup can swim and dive as soon as it is born.

 **Common seals**

Grey Seal

The grey seal's hair varies from pale grey or brown with no spots to much darker brown with large black splodges. Its head is large, with a long muzzle. The male is half as big again as the female.

Inset: The newly born grey seal pup is kept warm by its thick white coat, and does not swim until it has moulted.

Grey seals

From September to December the females come ashore, usually on rocky, uninhabited shores or islands, to have a single baby. The mother stays ashore for two or three weeks, feeding her white-coated pup on rich, fatty milk. She then leaves it to fend for itself. The pup, which by then has moulted its white coat, has to find its way to the sea and must learn to catch its own food.

Generally grey seals feed on fish, including sand eels, cod and whiting, but they will also eat squid and octopus.

Above: The grey seal's distinctive muzzle helps to distinguish it from the common seal.

Red Deer

The red deer is reddish-brown with a creamy patch on its rump. Nearly all male red deer, or stags, grow antlers, but they are cast (fall out) every year. The antlers are shaped rather like branches, and as a stag gets older its antlers become more and more branched. Stags that never grow antlers are called hummels in Scotland, and notts in South-west England.

Red deer browse on deciduous trees, grasses and rushes. The breeding season, called the rut, lasts from the end of September to November. During this time stags call to attract females, or hinds, and their loud roaring sounds can often be heard a long way away.

In May or June the hind gives birth, usually to a single calf. It is quite common to see a family group together, consisting of a hind, her young calf and a yearling born the previous summer.

Red deer that live in parks grow larger than those living on open hills in Scotland.

Right: The growing antlers of this red deer are covered in a hairy skin, which is called 'velvet'. When the antlers are fully grown, the velvet is rubbed off.

■ **Red deer**

Fallow Deer

Fallow deer are a reddish-fawn colour with white spots in summer, and greyish without spots in winter. The males, called bucks, have broad antlers. They usually walk or trot but when alarmed they will bound away, springing on all four feet. Bucks and does (females) live in separate herds most of the year, only getting together to mate. A single baby, or fawn, is born in June.

Fallow deer like grass for grazing or forest with undergrowth for sheltering and browsing. Usually they feed at dawn and dusk, resting and chewing the cud during the day.

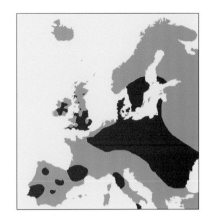

■ **Fallow deer**

Left: A fallow deer fawn can walk as soon as it is born.

Roe Deer

■ **Roe deer**

Roe deer have a short body and long legs with what appears to be just a tuft of hair rather than a tail. They stand very upright, and have pointed ears. The buck has small antlers. When alarmed, roe deer fluff up the paler hair on their rump. They enjoy eating the buds and shoots of trees and shrubs, and also eat some grass. The doe gives birth in May or June, often to twins. The doe keeps her fawns hidden at first, and returns to their hiding place regularly to suckle them.

Above: Unlike most other deer, roe deer are not usually seen in very large groups.

Domesticated Mammals

People learned to domesticate mammals long ago, in order to keep them for their milk or meat, and use their skin to make clothes. We still depend on these mammals in many ways.

Cattle

There were once wild cattle in Britain, but they became extinct around 2,500 years ago. The small Kerry cow is probably most like our earliest domesticated cow. Modern British Friesian cows give more milk, but need specially produced extra-high-energy foods.

Above: Jersey cows produce rich milk, which is ideal for making butter.

Left: This Suffolk sheep has a tight fleece of fine wool, good for a cold area with little rain.

Sheep

All domesticated sheep are descended from wild sheep that lived in Asia thousands of years ago. Today there are many different varieties, or breeds, and they live in different areas. For example, the blackface sheep of Scotland have long, coarse wool and are very hardy. In winter they can dig through snow to find grass to eat.

Pigs

Until the Middle Ages, domesticated pigs looked very like wild boar. The modern breeds that we know today were developed later. The best-known breed in Britain is the large white. At one time many people living in the countryside kept one in their back yard.

Horses and Ponies

Small, hardy, half-wild ponies have probably lived on Exmoor in the South-west of England since before the last Ice Age ended, around 10,000 years ago. Half-wild ponies can also be seen on Dartmoor and in the New Forest.

In the past, various breeds have been used as war horses, pack horses and as working farm animals. Today people still train ponies and horses to work in different ways, but most are kept as pets to be ridden.

Above: These pigs are about to be sold at a market.

Below: A foal on Dartmoor.

Pet and Feral Mammals

Left: Unlike most pets, cats are allowed to roam free. They often hunt for prey, even though they are well-fed at home.

Cats
People probably first tamed cats and kept them to kill mice and rats in food stores. All domesticated cats are thought to be descended from Asian wild cats.

Dogs
All of the domesticated dogs that we know today were originally bred from wolves. For centuries, dogs have helped people to herd and to hunt. Nowadays, some dogs are still used by people for herding sheep, as guard dogs, and as guide dogs for the blind. Dogs are extremely good companions, and are most common now as family pets.

Above: Dogs can be trained to understand many signals and work well with people.

People
There are more people than any other mammal in Britain, except the field vole. Like other mammal parents, people keep their young clean, warm and fed, and teach them until they can look after themselves. There are other similarities, too. When people lock their houses, they are defending their 'territory'. All mammals use scent to send messages, especially in courtship; people use perfume to make themselves attractive.

Feral cats and wildcats

Animals that have escaped to live and breed in the wild are called 'feral'. There are thousands of feral cats, which have run away or been abandoned. They live in small colonies, often in empty houses and sheds, farm outbuildings and dockyards. They survive by hunting small mammals and birds and by feeding on scraps.

True wildcats were widespread in Britain until the fifteenth century. As their forest homes were cut down and they were hunted for their fur, wildcats nearly became extinct. Now they are protected by law, but they live only in remote parts of Scotland.

Small Pet Mammals

Most of our favourite pets are mammals. Not only cats and dogs, but also guinea-pigs, gerbils, hamsters, rats and mice make popular pets.

Above: The wildcat has a thick, blunt-tipped tail.

Below: A pet hamster in its cage.

Be a Mammal Detective

We can often tell where wild mammals live and feed by the signs they leave behind. For example, look for burrows and holes in river banks, and runways in long grass.

Mammal Tracks

On soft ground or after snow, look carefully to see which mammals have passed. Make drawings of the mammal tracks you find, noting the place and date you found them. Notice the difference between tracks of front feet and hind feet. From the spacing of the tracks, try to work out whether the animal was moving slowly or quickly.

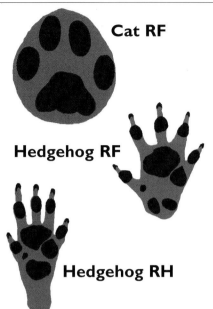

Cat RF

Hedgehog RF

Hedgehog RH

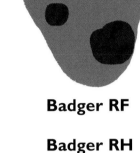

Badger RF

Badger RH

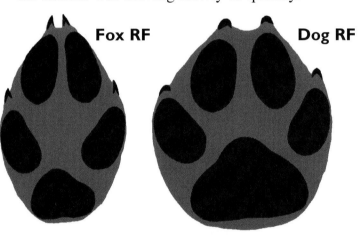

Fox RF   **Dog RF**

The tracks illustrated here are shown life size. RF means that the track was made by the animal's right front foot; RH means the right hind (back) foot.

Plaster casts

You could build up a collection of mammal footprints by making plaster casts.

To make a plaster cast you will need:
- a strip of card about 5 cm wide
- paper clips
- an old 500 g margarine tub
- plaster of Paris
- a tablespoon
- water
- a stick or spoon for stirring
- newspaper
- a trowel

1 Clear away grass or leaves around the footprint.
2 Make a circular 'wall' out of the piece of card, by fixing the ends together with a paper clip. Place the card circle over the print.
3 Mix about 5 heaped tablespoons of plaster with water in the margarine tub. The mixture should feel like smooth cream.
4 Pour the mixture into the card circle. Wait for about 15–30 minutes for the plaster to set.
5 Dig out the cast and the card. Wrap the cast in newspaper, take it home, clean it carefully and label it.

Droppings

Watch out for mammal droppings, which are often left in obvious places in order to mark an animal's territory. All rodent droppings are very hard. Bat droppings crumble easily because they are made up of undigested insect parts.

These droppings are all shown life size.

Common rat

Pipistrelle bat

Wood mouse

House mouse

Field vole

Rabbit

Hedgehog

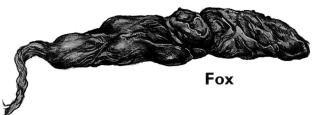

Fox

Badger

Food clues

Chewed food and leftovers are also good clues to help us identify mammals that have passed by. Hazel nuts are a popular food for a number of mammals, and it is often possible to tell which creature has been eating a hazel nut by the marks it has left on the shell.

Dormouse A smooth inner rim; tooth marks at an angle on the outer surface (right).

Wood mouse Parallel marks on the inner rim; rough marks on the outer surface (left).

Bank vole Parallel marks on the inner rim; no marks on the outer surface (right).

Squirrel Shells cracked open, leaving jagged edges on soft, unripe clusters (left); hardened nuts prised apart (right).

Spruce cone eaten by squirrel

Spruce cone eaten by wood mouse

Making Homes for Mammals

A hedgehog shelter

Gardens are important to hedgehogs for both food and shelter in summer. Hedgehogs also need a safe place to make a hibernation nest in winter. If you build a hedgehog house like the one below in an undisturbed corner, you may be lucky enough to have a lodger, especially if you know that hedgehogs already visit the area. Remember not to disturb a hedgehog when it is hibernating.

Never use wood that has been treated with chemicals – wood preservative or woodworm treatment fluid, for example.

When the box is ready, cover it with a sheet of heavy polythene, and put a mound of soil and leaves over it. Make sure the ventilation tube is not covered.

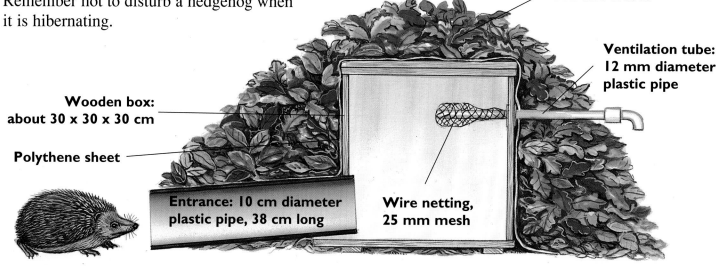

Soil and leaves

**Ventilation tube:
12 mm diameter
plastic pipe**

**Wooden box:
about 30 x 30 x 30 cm**

Polythene sheet

**Entrance: 10 cm diameter
plastic pipe, 38 cm long**

**Wire netting,
25 mm mesh**

Bat boxes

Ask an adult to help you build one or two bat boxes and fix them high up on trees. The wood should be at least 25 mm thick, rough sawn rather than planed smooth, and must not have been treated with chemicals.

Never try to saw wood without the help of an adult.

20 cm

36 cm

85 mm

14 cm

**Entrance gap:
15–18 mm**

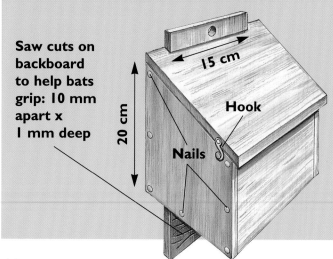

Saw cuts on backboard to help bats grip: 10 mm apart x 1 mm deep

15 cm

20 cm

Hook

Nails

The entrance gap at the bottom of each box should be 15 mm – 18 mm wide; don't make it wider. Site the box where the sun will warm it for as long as possible. If bats do come to live in your boxes, make sure you don't disturb them.

Mammal Watching

There are a number of things you can do that will help you to watch mammals without disturbing them.

Plants for bats
If you grow night-scented plants, such as honeysuckle, they will attract the insects that bats eat. Dusk is the best time to watch for bats feeding.

Make a food table
If you have a garden you could build a food table like the one in the picture for voles and mice. Ask an adult to help you do this. Make a safe pathway to it with branches and protect the table with chicken wire: use wire of 4 cm mesh – the holes are large enough for the mice and voles to get through but too small for predators.

Put food on the table just before dusk: try raisins, seeds and nuts, apples and peanut butter. Look for mammal droppings and food remains in the morning.

Food table

Hide and see
Make a 'hide' and watch your visitors on warm summer evenings. You could use an old blanket draped over a clothes horse or over pieces of wood tied together.

When you are going to watch, wear dark clothes. Tape a red filter (made from a transparent red sweet wrapper or a piece of thin red plastic) over the front of your torch. This will help you to see the animals without them being able to see you. Be in place in your hide before dusk, keep very quiet and be patient! Keep a note in a mammal notebook of everything that you see.

Mammal behaviour at home
Watch kittens and puppies learning to hunt through play – chasing and pouncing.

Watch a cat rubbing against walls, furniture and people. It is marking its territory.

Watch cows that are lying down return cud to their mouth, chew it, then swallow (see page 38).

Watch your family and friends too!

Right: When watching for mammals, try to keep downwind of where you expect to see them, so they cannot smell you.

Glossary

Aggressive Quarrelsome and prone to fighting.

Blubber A thick layer of fat just under the skin of a seal or other sea mammal.

Browse To feed on twigs and the young shoots of trees.

Chewing the cud Bringing back up and chewing food that has already been swallowed.

Colony A group of animals of one species living close together.

Coniferous trees Evergreen trees such as pines and firs that produce cones.

Crops Plants, such as wheat and barley, that are grown by farmers.

Deciduous trees Trees such as oak and ash that shed their leaves in autumn.

Diet The kind of food an animal eats.

Domesticate To tame an animal in order for it to live with humans, as a pet or livestock.

Dorsal On the back.

Echolocation A system of locating or finding objects using sound.

Extinct A word describing a species that has died out completely.

Flanks The sides of the body between ribs and hips.

Flexible Able to bend without breaking.

Foraging Searching for food.

Gnaw To wear away by biting.

Graze To eat growing grass.

Habitat The place where a plant or animal lives naturally.

Hibernate To spend winter in an inactive state.

Invertebrates Animals without backbones; worms and insects, for example.

Mammary gland The gland in female mammals which produces milk.

Marine To do with the sea. Marine mammals, such as seals and dolphins, live in the sea.

Membrane In bats, a double layer of skin.

Muzzle The jaws and mouth of a mammal.

Native Belonging naturally to a place.

Nocturnal Active at night.

Pest An animal that causes a nuisance, usually by eating or damaging crops.

Pesticides Substances used to kill animals that eat or damage crops.

Polluted Made dirty, sometimes by chemicals.

Predator An animal that hunts and kills other animals for food.

Prey An animal that is hunted and killed by another for food.

Roost A place a bird or bat settles to rest.

Sociable When an animal or person likes being with others.

Sonar A system for finding your way around using sound.

Species A group of animals or plants that are all similar and can breed with each other.

Suckle To drink milk from a mammary gland.

Territory An area which an animal or group of animals claims as its own, and will defend against others of the same species.

Weaned When an animal is able to eat food other than its mother's milk.

Left: Magpies picking insects from the coat of a red deer.

Books to Read

Animals of Britain (Readers Digest Nature Lover's Library, 1996)

Care for the Badger (Care for the Wild International)

Mammals by David Burnie (Dorling Kindersley Explorers, 1997)

Field Guide to the Mammals of Britain and Europe by John Burton (Kingfisher Books, 1991)

Amazing Mammals (Dorling Kindersley Junior Eyewitness series, 1998)

Mammal by Steve Parker (Dorling Kindersley Eyewitness Guide, 1989). This book is superbly illustrated and packed with information on the behaviour and anatomy of mammals. A video of this title is also available.

How to Find and Identify Mammals by Gillie Sargent and Pat Morris (Mammal Society, 1997)

Mammal Detective by Rob Strachan (Whittet Books, 1995)

Whittet Books have published a series of books on individual mammals, including *Bats, Badgers, Squirrels, Seals, Rabbits and Hares, Otters,* and *Mice and Voles.*

Mammal-watcher's code

- Never go out alone, especially at night.
- Always tell someone exactly where you are going, and how long you expect to be.
- Always ask permission before going on private land, and tell the owner what you found.
- The animals come first: avoid disturbing them.
- Respect the habitat you are exploring.
- Don't drop any litter or damage plants.
- Close gates and keep to the edge of crop fields.

Find out more about the marvellous world of mammals

The Mammal Society 15 Cloisters House, 8 Battersea Park Road, London SW8 4BG. Send a SAE for a list of publications and details of the Youth Group – Mammalaction – and local groups.
Website: www.abdn.ac.uk/mammal

The Bat Conservation Trust
15 Cloisters House, 8 Battersea Park Road, London SW8 4BG. Send a SAE for more information and details of the junior section – The Young Batworker's Club – and local groups. Website: www.bats.org.uk

National Federation of Badger Groups
15 Cloisters House, 8 Battersea Park Road, London SW8 4BG.

Whale and Dolphin Conservation Society Alexander House, James Street West, Bath BA1 2BT Tel: 01225 334511 Website: www.wdcs.org/wdcs/index.htm

WWF UK Panda House, Weyside Park, Godalming, Surrey GU7 1XR
Tel: 01483 426444
Website: www.wwf-uk.org

Index